NATIONAL GEOGRAPHIC | **GLOBAL ISSUES**

FOOD SUPPLY

Andrew J. Milson, Ph.D.
Content Consultant
University of Texas at Arlington

Acknowledgments

Grateful acknowledgment is given to the authors, artists, photographers, museums, publishers, and agents for permission to reprint copyrighted material. Every effort has been made to secure the appropriate permission. If any omissions have been made or if corrections are required, please contact the Publisher.

Instructional Consultant: Christopher Johnson, Evanston, Illinois

Teacher Reviewers: Leah Perry, Exploris Middle School, Raleigh, North Carolina
Erin Stevens, Quabbin Regional Middle/High School, Barre, Massachusetts

Photographic Credits

Cover, Inside Front Cover, Title Page ©Keren Su/Corbis. **3** (bg) ©David Toase/Stockbyte/Getty Images. **4** (bg) ©Steve Winter/National Geographic Stock. **6** (bg) ©REUTERS/Finbarr O'Reilly. **7** (tl) ©Jake Lyell/Alamy. **8** (bg) Mapping Specialists. **10** (bg) ©Jamie Marshall/Tribaleye Images/Getty Images. **11** (bl) Mapping Specialists. **12** (bg) ©Matiullah Achakza/epa/Corbis. **14** (tr) ©Arshad Arbab/epa/Corbis. **15** (bg) ©Farooq Naeem/AFP/Getty Images. **16** (t) ©REUTERS/Ismail Taxta. **17** (br) ©Boris Roessler/epa/Corbis. **19** (bg) ©REUTERS/Feisal Omar. **21** (bg) ©REUTERS/Omar Faruk. (tl) ©REUTERS/Feisal Omar. **22** (bg) ©Marshall Burke. **23** (tl) ©Zacharie Sero Tamou. **24** (cr) ©Lennart Woltering. **25** (bg) ©Joerg Boethling/Alamy. **27** (t) ©Gage/Getty Images. **28** (tl) ©Gary K Smith/Garden Picture Library/Getty Images. **30** (br) ©Jake Lyell/Alamy. (tr) ©Janet Jarman/Corbis News/Corbis. **31** (bg) ©David Toase/Stockbyte/Getty Images. (tr) ©James P. Blair/National Geographic Stock. (bl) ©Edwin Remsberg/Getty Images. (br) ©REUTERS/Stringer.

MetaMetrics® and the MetaMetrics logo and tagline are trademarks of MetaMetrics, Inc., and are registered in the United States and abroad. The trademarks and names of other companies and products mentioned herein are the property of their respective owners. Copyright © 2010 MetaMetrics, Inc. All rights reserved.

Visit National Geographic Learning online at www.NGSP.com.

Visit our corporate website at www.cengage.com.

Printed in the USA.

RR Donnelley, Menasha, WI

ISBN: 978-07362-97585

13 14 15 16 17 18 19 20 21 22

10 9 8 7 6 5 4 3 2

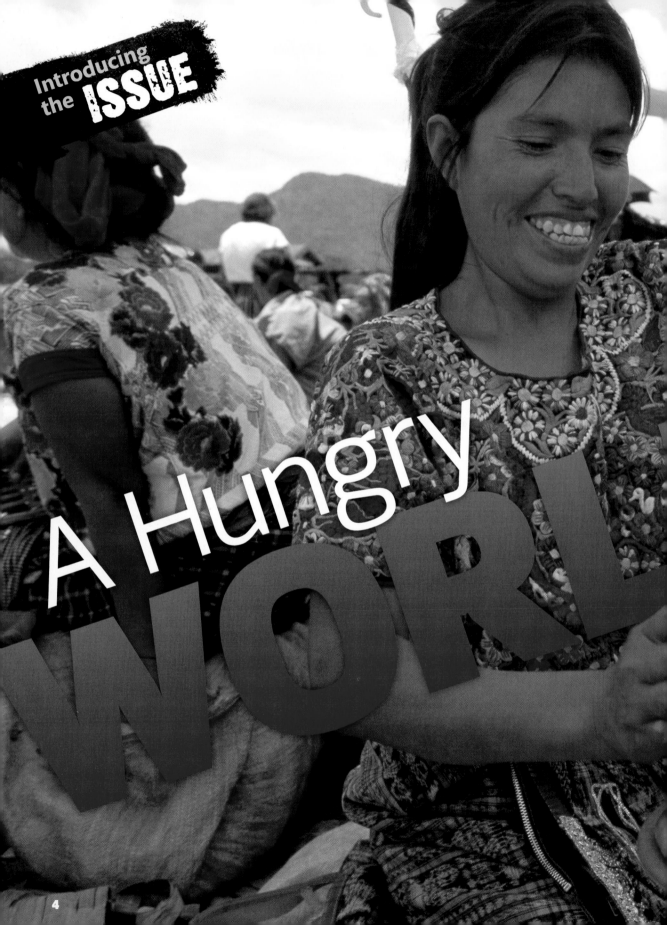

A Hungry WORL

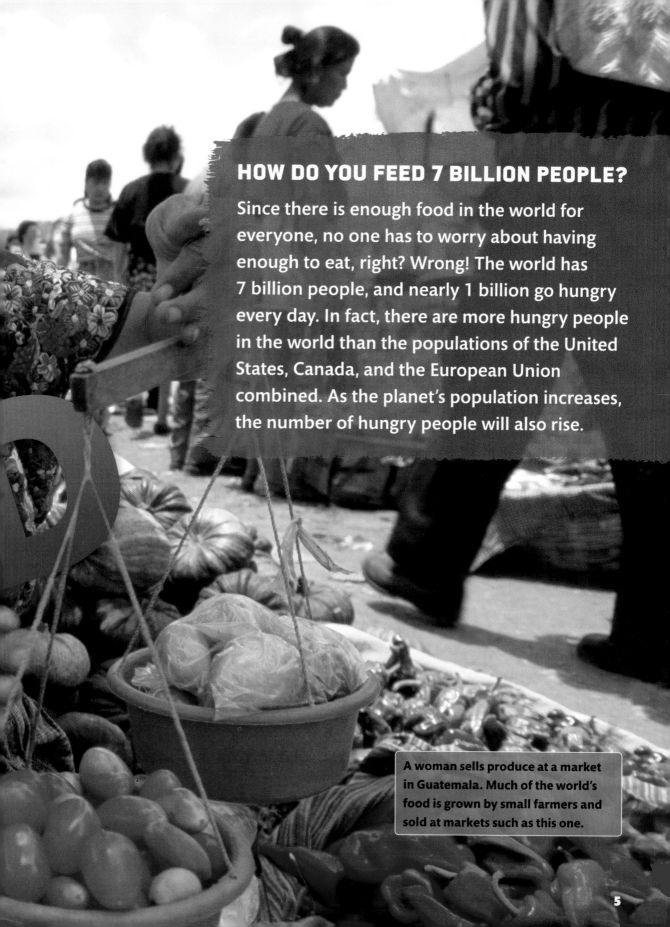

HOW DO YOU FEED 7 BILLION PEOPLE?

Since there is enough food in the world for everyone, no one has to worry about having enough to eat, right? Wrong! The world has 7 billion people, and nearly 1 billion go hungry every day. In fact, there are more hungry people in the world than the populations of the United States, Canada, and the European Union combined. As the planet's population increases, the number of hungry people will also rise.

A woman sells produce at a market in Guatemala. Much of the world's food is grown by small farmers and sold at markets such as this one.

FOOD IS LIFE

For thousands of years, people all over the world have practiced **agriculture**, the raising of food. Farmers work the soil to grow crops such as corn, beans, or melons. They raise animals for meat or to provide milk. Some farmers plant trees that produce fruit, nuts, coffee beans, or tea leaves.

Without food, you could not survive. Food gives you energy and helps you stay healthy. Yet many people cannot afford enough food for themselves and their families. Others do not have land on which to grow the food they need.

More than a thousand women and children wait for emergency food aid in a village in Niger, western Africa. Drought and natural disasters can leave millions hungry. Various organizations worldwide work to feed people in situations like this.

Children receive food aid in Malawi, southern Africa.

EMPTY FOOD BOWLS

Even people who have the skills to grow their own food can be at risk of starving. Small farmers are often poor. When their crops fail or sell at low prices, they go hungry.

Sometimes food in a region becomes extremely scarce. This scarcity is called **famine**. It can lead to starvation and even death. When a region's major food crops fail, famine is a very real danger. Crops can fail for a number of reasons, including poor soil and **drought**—a long period without rain. Plant diseases, insects, extreme weather, and war can also destroy crops and create famine.

Some poor people live in **food deserts**, areas where stores that sell nutritious foods are too far away to reach easily. A food desert can be in the middle of a bustling city, or it can be out in the country. Even in times of plenty, people living in a food desert are at risk of going hungry. They may also suffer from certain diseases because the only easily available food is not healthful.

WHERE'S DINNER?

Making sure the world's people have enough to eat involves new ways of thinking about food supply. In cities, for example, people have begun growing food in their yards and even on their roofs. In remote rural areas, people are working to increase food yields by making the most of soil and water resources.

In the following pages you will read about how people in Pakistan and Somalia are working to build **food security**—continued access to sufficient and nutritious food.

Explore the Issue

1. **Identify** What is agriculture? How do the various aspects of agriculture contribute to the world's food supply?

2. **Analyze Cause and Effect** What factors contribute to the fact that 1 billion people do not have enough food?

Hunger in Our

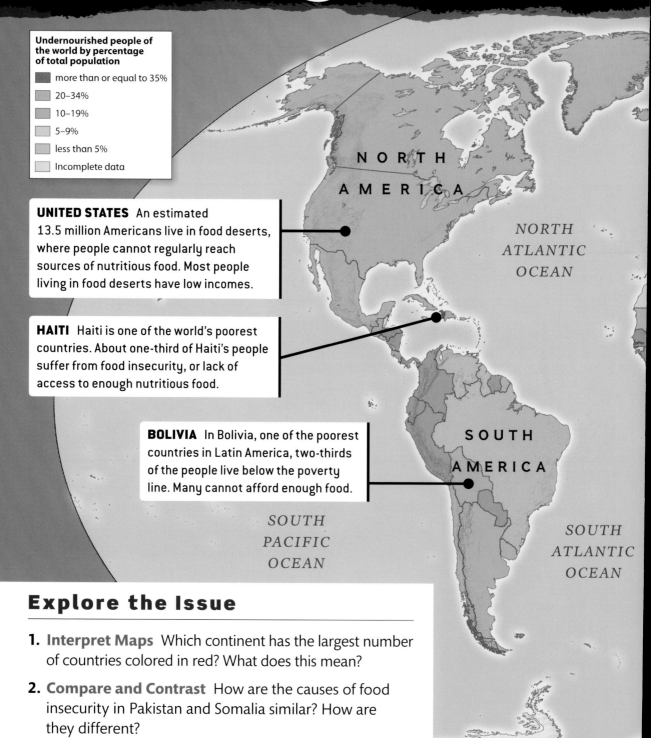

Undernourished people of the world by percentage of total population

- more than or equal to 35%
- 20–34%
- 10–19%
- 5–9%
- less than 5%
- Incomplete data

UNITED STATES An estimated 13.5 million Americans live in food deserts, where people cannot regularly reach sources of nutritious food. Most people living in food deserts have low incomes.

HAITI Haiti is one of the world's poorest countries. About one-third of Haiti's people suffer from food insecurity, or lack of access to enough nutritious food.

BOLIVIA In Bolivia, one of the poorest countries in Latin America, two-thirds of the people live below the poverty line. Many cannot afford enough food.

NORTH AMERICA

NORTH ATLANTIC OCEAN

SOUTH AMERICA

SOUTH PACIFIC OCEAN

SOUTH ATLANTIC OCEAN

Explore the Issue

1. **Interpret Maps** Which continent has the largest number of countries colored in red? What does this mean?

2. **Compare and Contrast** How are the causes of food insecurity in Pakistan and Somalia similar? How are they different?

World

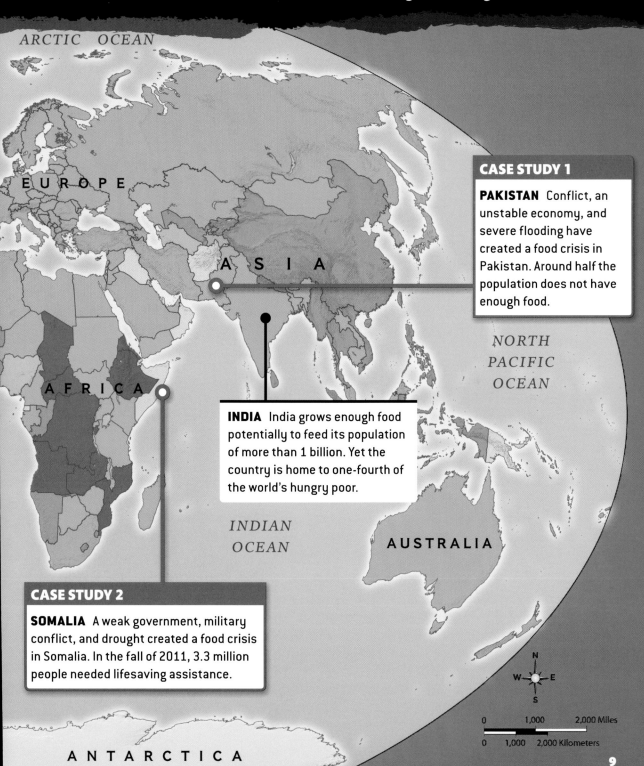

ARCTIC OCEAN

EUROPE

ASIA

AFRICA

NORTH PACIFIC OCEAN

INDIAN OCEAN

AUSTRALIA

ANTARCTICA

CASE STUDY 1

PAKISTAN Conflict, an unstable economy, and severe flooding have created a food crisis in Pakistan. Around half the population does not have enough food.

INDIA India grows enough food potentially to feed its population of more than 1 billion. Yet the country is home to one-fourth of the world's hungry poor.

CASE STUDY 2

SOMALIA A weak government, military conflict, and drought created a food crisis in Somalia. In the fall of 2011, 3.3 million people needed lifesaving assistance.

N
W — E
S

0   1,000   2,000 Miles

0   1,000   2,000 Kilometers

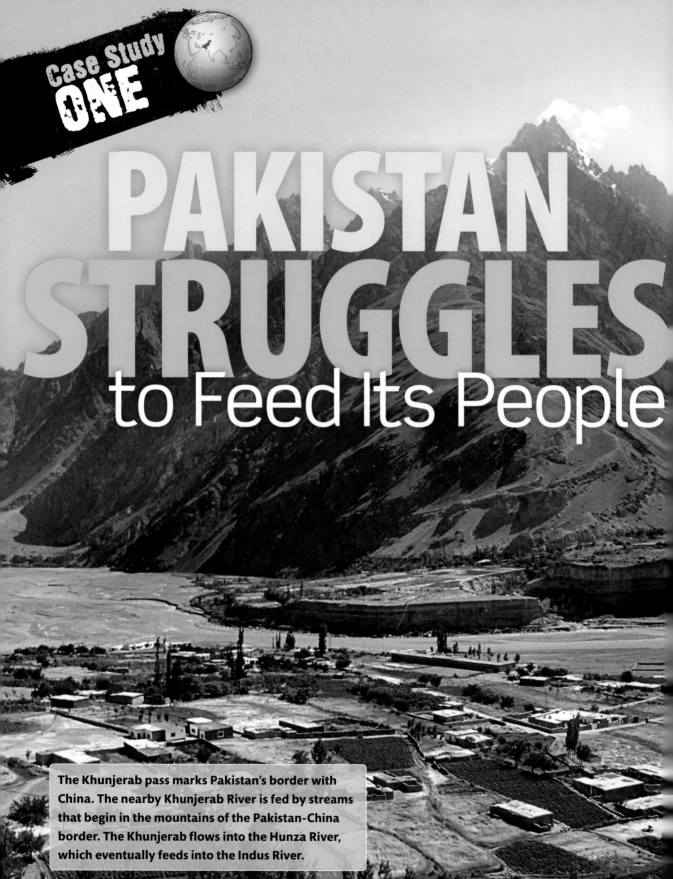

PAKISTAN STRUGGLES
to Feed Its People

The Khunjerab pass marks Pakistan's border with China. The nearby Khunjerab River is fed by streams that begin in the mountains of the Pakistan-China border. The Khunjerab flows into the Hunza River, which eventually feeds into the Indus River.

SEEKING HIGHER GROUND

In September 2011, a man waded through waist-deep water in Pakistan. His name was Kaywall, and he was carrying a goat. Since floodwaters had destroyed his home, Kaywall spent two weeks moving his goats to higher ground. The goats were all that was left of his family's belongings. "My house was destroyed," Kaywall told a reporter. He and his family were stranded by high water.

Kaywall was not the only one struggling to salvage something from his home. His entire village was under water because of floods that had devastated parts of Pakistan.

A LONG HISTORY

Kaywall's experience shows the challenges that face many people in Pakistan today. Established in 1947, the country represents a new chapter in the long history of the Indus Valley in South Asia. About five thousand years ago, a great civilization arose along the Indus River, which runs from north to south through what is now Pakistan. This civilization, the Indus Valley civilization, was urban, with Harappa (huh-RAP-puh) and Mohenjo Daro (moh-HEN-joh DA-roh) its major cities.

The Indus Valley was green, forested, and fertile because of the area's geography. Water flowing down from the melting snows atop high mountain ranges fed the streams that joined to form the Indus River. Seasonal rains also contributed to the river's flow. The Indus people learned to use the rich land and plentiful water to feed themselves. They were among the first humans to develop the techniques of agriculture.

In the modern state of Pakistan, the situation is very different. The Indus River still flows through the mountains and receives water from snowmelt and seasonal rains. However, natural disasters and other factors have disrupted agriculture. In 2009, 83 million people—nearly half of Pakistan's population—suffered from food insecurity.

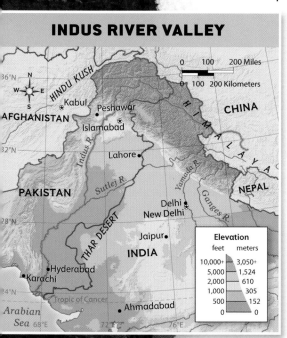

This map shows the course of the Indus River through Pakistan. Note that the river crosses high mountains over much of its path.

People struggle to leave flooded areas in Punjab Province in August 2010.

THEN CAME THE FLOODS

Weather disasters are one cause of Pakistan's food insecurity. One of the most destructive of these occurred in 2010, when Pakistan experienced the worst floods in its history.

Monsoons (mahn-SOONZ) are the seasonal rains that bring much-needed water to Pakistan's crops. Monsoons are a mixed blessing. Farmers welcome the rains, because their crops need the water. However, sometimes monsoons bring too much rain—more than the land can absorb. In 2010, the rains were greater than usual. They caused rivers to swell and flood, destroying homes and crops. Millions had no access to food or safe drinking water. Many farmers were unable to plant spring wheat.

The following year, heavy monsoons again brought disaster. Sources disagree on the precise numbers, but by October 2011, flooding had affected between 5 and 10 million people. It had destroyed more than 2 million acres of crops. Over 112,000 **livestock**—animals being raised for meat or milk—were killed by the flooding. An additional 5 million animals were at risk.

The events of 2010 and 2011 may indicate an alarming trend. Recent evidence suggests that the monsoon nucleus, or center, may have shifted from India to Pakistan. Such a shift would bring a repeat of the heavy monsoon rains for at least 20 years.

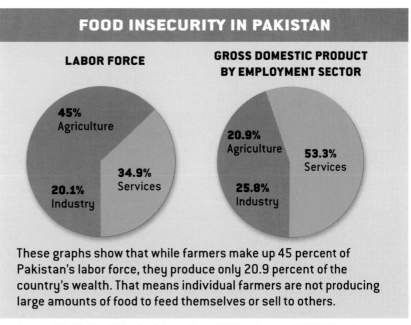

FOOD INSECURITY IN PAKISTAN

LABOR FORCE

45% Agriculture
34.9% Services
20.1% Industry

GROSS DOMESTIC PRODUCT BY EMPLOYMENT SECTOR

20.9% Agriculture
53.3% Services
25.8% Industry

These graphs show that while farmers make up 45 percent of Pakistan's labor force, they produce only 20.9 percent of the country's wealth. That means individual farmers are not producing large amounts of food to feed themselves or sell to others.

Source: CIA, *The World Factbook*, labor force 2010 estimates; GDP 2011 estimates

RISING COSTS, RISING HUNGER

Social and economic factors also contribute to Pakistan's food insecurity. These include inflation and unequal land ownership. **Inflation**, or rising prices, can put basic food items out of reach for the poor. Throughout 2010, the cost of wheat and rice rose 30–50 percent in Pakistan.

Unequal land distribution is another issue. Just 2 percent of the households in Pakistan control almost half the land. Many others have little land, if any, on which to grow food.

Emergency food was supplied for flood victims in Peshawar in September 2010.

SOLVING PAKISTAN'S FOOD PROBLEMS

The problem of hunger in Pakistan is not an easy one to solve. Experts have proposed a wide range of solutions. One idea is to plant a greater variety of crops, including crops that need less water and provide more nutrition.

Another suggestion is to improve **infrastructure**, such as roads, bridges, and the dams that regulate water in the irrigation systems. Better roads and bridges would make it easier and cheaper for farmers to transport their crops to markets. Better irrigation dams would mean a more even distribution of water over farm fields.

To help Pakistani farmers improve their skills—and grow more food—aid agencies have set up farmer field schools. At these schools, farmers learn how to defeat diseases and pests. They also learn how to prepare land for planting and how to choose seeds that are right for their soil. These field schools are helping Pakistan's farmers create a brighter future for themselves.

Explore the Issue

1. **Find Main Ideas** What are the two major contributing factors to Pakistan's food insecurity?

2. **Evaluate** Look at the possible solutions to Pakistan's hunger problems. Which do you think will be most effective? Explain.

In December 2010, Pakistani farmers plant onions in a formerly flooded field in the Swat Valley. Like the Indus, the Swat is a river fed by water from the nearby mountains.

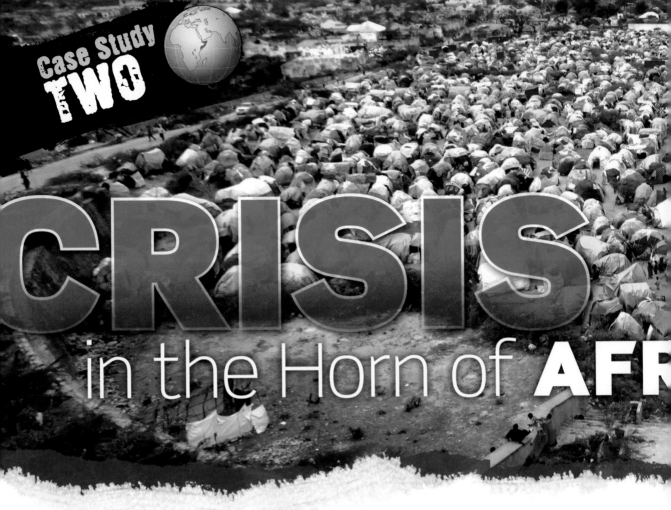

CRISIS
in the Horn of AFR

FIGHTING AGAINST FAMINE

In the summer of 2011, tens of thousands of people in Somalia, Ethiopia, Djibouti (jib-BOO-tee), Kenya, and Uganda were dying. It was the world's worst food crisis. The five affected countries are located at the eastern tip of Africa, an area called the Horn of Africa.

Hunger drove people to abandon their homes in search of food. An estimated 450,000 people made their way to a refugee camp in Dadaab (duh-DAHB), Kenya. Among them was Aden, a three-year-old boy from Somalia. He and his family had walked for 25 days to reach the camp. On the way, his mother died. When Aden arrived at the camp, he was close to death from **malnutrition**, a lack of adequate food. Aden's father took him to the camp's nutrition center, where he received treatment. For a month, Aden's father never left his side. Gradually, Aden recovered. He and his family remained at the camp. They had nowhere else to go.

Seyidka, near Somalia's capital Mogadishu, is a settlement for people driven from their homes by famine.

CA

STARVING IN SOMALIA

Of the countries experiencing famine, Somalia was the most severely affected. Drought caused shortages of food and water. Around 4 million people—half of Somalia's population—were hungry.

Many people in Somalia make their living by raising livestock. Drought dries up the **pasture**, or grazing land, that provides food for the animals. As a result, many animals die, and the people who raise them lose not just their **livelihood**—the way they support themselves—but their way of life.

A family of Somalian refugees find shelter in Dadaab in August 2011.

In the summer of 2011, 75,000 Somalis sought relief in Dadaab. By fall, aid groups were still trying to reach millions of people in danger of starving. Nobody knows for sure how many children were at risk of dying.

THE WORST DROUGHT IN 60 YEARS

The drought in East Africa was the worst in 60 years. In Somalia, drought and **desertification** (dih-zur-tuh-fa-KAY-shuhn) combined to increase the threat of famine. Desertification occurs when productive land in an arid or semiarid climate becomes too dry or desertlike to be fertile.

In Somalia, the loss of trees was a primary cause of desertification. People burned forests to create charcoal to sell. With fewer trees to block the wind, soil erosion increased.

Somalia's problems are also political. In 1991, rebels overthrew the government. Since then, different groups have fought a long civil war for control of the country. As a result, Somalia has had a weak central government. It has been unable to afford programs to improve agriculture and irrigation. In 2009, a military group called al-Shabab (AL-shah-bahb) forced aid agencies to leave a number of areas where they were trying to bring food to the population, leaving people to go hungry. As a BBC News report on Africa stated, "Basically, conflict turns drought into famine."

RELIEF AND HARDSHIP

In October 2011, rains fell in south central Somalia, where drought in some areas had lasted as long as two years. People could once again plant crops.

The rains also brought more suffering, however. In refugee camps in and around Mogadishu (moh-guh-DEE-shoo), Somalia's capital, people were living in makeshift huts of cardboard, sticks, and plastic sheeting. When the rains came, the flimsy huts fell apart. As a result, hundreds of thousands of displaced people were left without shelter.

The rains also made it more difficult to distribute aid, while at the same time increasing the risk of cholera and other waterborne diseases. Risk of disease is greatest among people who are weak and undernourished, especially children. Crowded conditions in the camps further increased the risk.

In Somalia, malaria threatened millions of people. Mosquitoes, the insects that carry malaria, require water to breed. In the wetter conditions, the number of mosquitoes multiplied rapidly.

"Basically, conflict turns a drought into a famine."

—BBC News report on Africa

Civil war in Somalia has resulted in the destruction of many homes. This wrecked building is in Kaaran district, south of Mogadishu.

COMBATING FAMINE

The crisis in Somalia called for immediate solutions: feed the hungry, provide shelter, and care for the sick. Long-term solutions were equally important to prevent similar crises in the future.

International organizations began developing systems to manage drought and to stop desertification. They recommended that drought-prone countries such as Somalia improve the way they monitor droughts and share information.

Environmental organizations have worked to slow desertification and improve agricultural productivity. One effort has reduced the amount of charcoal exported from Somalia. Another plan aims to introduce bee keeping to help farmers increase their income and provide greater food security.

Aid agencies have provided farmers with seeds for growing several crops, including corn. Farmers have also received fertilizers and tools for improving their **yield**—the amount of food they can grow per acre. Aid agencies have helped rebuild roads and irrigation channels that were destroyed in Somalia's civil war.

PEACE MAY BRING RELIEF

Many believe that efforts should focus not just on international aid for Somalia's people but on making the government strong and stable. Experts hope that a strong central government will be able to end the fighting and bring peace to the country. With the conflicts ended, the people of Somalia could focus on rebuilding their homes and farms. The solution to hunger in Somalia will not come only from international aid. With a peaceful, stable government, the Somalis themselves can work toward preventing famine in the future.

Explore the Issue

1. **Analyze Causes** What factors are making it hard for the Somalis to feed their people?

2. **Contrast** In what ways are the proposed solutions to hunger in Somalia and Pakistan different? Explain why different ideas are being tried in the two countries.

A storekeeper sells food in Mogadishu, March 2010. Armed conflict in the Somali capital has made it hard for store owners to stay in business.

Somali workers unload aid supplies from Saudi Arabia for Somalia in August 2011.

A "Green" Approach to Relieving Hunger

A woman harvests lettuce during the dry season in Dunkassa, Benin. Solar powered drip irrigation has allowed people to grow nutritious vegetables during the long 8-month dry season.

FAR FROM SIMPLE

Environmental scientist Jennifer Burney worries that solutions to world hunger may contribute to a different problem—**climate change**, or the gradual warming of Earth's temperatures. In turn, climate change increases the challenge of defeating hunger.

Growing food can create pollution. Runoff water from irrigation may wash chemical fertilizers into lakes and streams. Tractors and other fuel-driven farm equipment produce greenhouse gases that heat up the planet.

As Earth warms, weather patterns become more irregular, making crops harder to grow. More frequent hurricanes and other strong storms cause intense rains. These heavy rains cause flooding.

Jennifer Burney works with villagers in Africa.

Progress and growth in agriculture can bring great benefits, creating a more plentiful and varied food supply. Yet the consequences of that progress, as you have just learned, can be harmful. As a National Geographic Emerging Explorer, Jennifer Burney is working with the Society to find a balance. She is striving to reduce hunger while protecting the environment. In sub-Saharan Africa, she works with poor farmers struggling to raise food. "We are a world of plenty, yet almost a billion people don't have enough to eat," notes Burney.

HARNESSING THE SUN

At a test site in Benin (BEH-nin) in West Africa, Burney has tapped into the sun's energy. With support from the Solar Electric Light Fund, she has helped set up solar-powered water pumps. These pumps regulate the amount of water the irrigation systems receive. On sunny days the pumps work faster, and on cloudy days they work slower. This ensures that the crops, which need more water on sunny days, get the amount of water they need. No fuel is burned to produce power, so no pollutants are released into the air.

Three years after its installation, the system has improved the farmers' lives. They are able to grow greater quantities of fruits and vegetables. They have more money to buy food and to send their children to school.

CLEANER COOKING

According to Burney, reducing the harmful effects of cooking on the environment is also important. Cooking uses about 8 percent of energy resources in the world. In developing nations, cooking is especially inefficient. Stoves traditionally used in these countries burn wood or dung, which create soot. When soot is released in homes, it can make people ill. Outside, soot can seriously harm the environment. Soot speeds up the melting of glaciers, alters monsoon cycles, and contributes to global warming.

In India, Burney is working to replace traditional cooking stoves with more efficient ones. Early results indicate that the eco-stoves are less polluting. They also require less fuel. Jennifer Burney believes that replacing traditional stoves will immediately begin slowing climate change.

MAKE A DIFFERENCE

There is no single solution to the problem of feeding the hungry. In each part of the world, different factors contribute to hunger. Each solution must be weighed against possible consequences.

You can join National Geographic in the search for solutions to hunger. First, learn all you can about the issues. Read up on how and where food is raised, nutrition, climate change, and other matters relating to hunger. Decisions made anywhere on Earth about food production and land use affect you, so understand what's happening.

You can also find ways to take action. The activity on the next two pages can help you be part of the solution to hunger in your own community.

Jennifer Burney and farmers in Bessassi, Benin, inspect the farmers' solar-powered water pumps.

Explore the Issue

1. **Analyze Causes** What is the relationship between agriculture and the environment?

2. **Identify Problems and Solutions** Why does Jennifer Burney believe that cooking with eco-stoves in developing nations can slow climate change?

"We are a world of plenty, yet almost a billion people don't have enough to eat." —Jennifer Burney

A woman in West Africa uses a solar cooker to prepare a meal. Unlike some traditional stoves, a solar cooker does not release harmful substances into the air.

Volunteer
at a Community
Garden
—and share your results

The solution to world hunger may begin at home. Get involved by volunteering at a community garden and raising fresh fruits and vegetables. The healthy food you grow will help feed hungry people in your part of the world.

IDENTIFY

- Research local community gardens that grow produce.

- Phone or visit the gardens you are interested in to find out about the different tasks you might be asked to do.

- Get the facts. Ask how much food the garden typically produces each year. Also ask how it is distributed to those who need it.

ORGANIZE

- Figure out how much time you can devote to the community garden each week. Then make a schedule.

- Gather whatever tools you'll need for your work in the garden, such as gloves, shovels, rakes, and trowels.

- Recruit friends and family members who are also willing to work in the community garden during the growing season.

A teacher and her students tend the garden they have planted at their school. These herbs and vegetables could help feed people in the community.

DOCUMENT

- Take photos before, during, and after work in the community garden. You might also shoot videos of work sessions.

- Keep a record of what is planted in the community garden. In addition, record the amount grown of each type of herb, fruit, or vegetable.

- Jot down your experiences with the plants, the work, and your fellow volunteers and note what you learned in a journal.

SHARE

- Use your photos and videos to create a multimedia presentation of the community garden project and show it to your class.

- Propose that your school start a community garden project that students can help organize and run.

- Write an article for your local paper describing your volunteer work and how it made a difference to you and your community.

Research & WRITE Explanatory

Write a How-To Guide

You have volunteered at a community garden in which you helped grow food. Draw on that experience and do some further research to write a how-to guide for others who wish to plant a garden. A clear, well-written gardening guide may inspire friends and family members to start growing food themselves.

RESEARCH

Use the Internet, books, and articles as well as your own experiences in a community garden to research and answer the following questions:

- What soil and sun conditions are best for growing produce in your community?
- When is the best planting time for these food crops?
- How much water and fertilizer do the plants need?

As you do your research, be sure to take notes. Check your sources for accuracy and credibility.

DRAFT

Review your notes and then write a first draft.

- Introduce your topic clearly, previewing what is to follow in your how-to guide.
- Use bullet points to list the steps in the gardening process. Develop the steps using relevant facts and concrete details from your experience in the garden.
- Use appropriate transitions to clarify the relationships among your ideas and the steps in the process.
- Inform your readers using precise language and vocabulary that is specific to gardening.
- In the last paragraph, provide a concluding statement that follows from and supports the information you presented in your introduction and step-by-step list.

REVISE & EDIT

Read your first draft to make sure that it provides step-by-step information on starting a garden.

- Do you clearly introduce the topic of your how-to guide?
- Do the steps contain helpful, relevant, and concrete information?
- Are the transitions between the steps clear and easy to follow?
- Do you use precise, gardening-specific language?
- Does your conclusion sum up and support the information and explanations in your guide?

Revise the how-to guide to make sure you have covered all the bases. Then check your paper for errors in spelling and punctuation.

PUBLISH & PRESENT

Now you are ready to publish and present your how-to guide. Add any images that may help explain the steps you describe. Then print out your guide or write a clean copy by hand. Consider placing the guide in your school library for others to use.

Visual GLOSSARY

agriculture

food security

agriculture *n.*, the growing of food

climate change *n.*, gradual changes in Earth's temperatures

desertification *n.*, the degrading of productive land to a less fertile, desert-like condition

drought *n.*, a long period without rain

famine *n.*, an extreme scarcity of food

food desert *n.*, a place where there is no nearby source of healthful food

food security *n.*, regular access to sufficient and nutritious food

inflation *n.*, rising prices for goods

infrastructure *n.*, permanent structures that are built for public use such as roads, bridges, railroads, dams, and irrigation systems

livelihood *n.*, the way a person earns his or her living

livestock *n.*, animals raised for meat or milk

malnutrition *n.*, poor health caused by a lack of adequate food

monsoon *n.*, seasonal rain of South Asia

pasture *n.*, land where animals can graze

yield *n.*, the amount of crops a piece of land can produce per acre

monsoons

drought

livestock

INDEX

SKILLS